HAL•LEONARD
INSTRUMENTAL
PLAY-ALONG

AUDIO ACCESS INCLUDED

PLAYBACK+
Speed • Pitch • Balance • Loop

CELLO

Christmas Carols

TITLE	PAGE
Christ Was Born on Christmas Day	2
Deck the Hall	3
The First Noel	4
Good Christian Men, Rejoice	6
Good King Wenceslas	7
Hark! The Herald Angels Sing	8
I Heard the Bells on Christmas Day	9
It Came Upon the Midnight Clear	10
Joy to the World	12
O Christmas Tree	14
O Come, O Come, Emmanuel	15
O Little Town of Bethlehem	22
Sing We Now of Christmas	16
We Three Kings of Orient Are	18
We Wish You a Merry Christmas	20

T0087792

To access audio visit:
www.halleonard.com/mylibrary

Enter Code
3401-7242-0999-8744

ISBN: 978-1-4234-1363-9

HAL•LEONARD®
CORPORATION
7777 W. BLUEMOUND RD. P.O. BOX 13819 MILWAUKEE, WI 53213

For all works contained herein:
Unauthorized copying, arranging, adapting, recording, Internet posting, public performance,
or other distribution of the printed or recorded music in this publication is an infringement of copyright.
Infringers are liable under the law.

Visit Hal Leonard Online at
www.halleonard.com

CHRIST WAS BORN ON CHRISTMAS DAY

CELLO

Traditional

Copyright © 2006 by HAL LEONARD CORPORATION
International Copyright Secured All Rights Reserved

DECK THE HALL

CELLO

Traditional Welsh Carol

Copyright © 2006 by HAL LEONARD CORPORATION
International Copyright Secured All Rights Reserved

THE FIRST NOEL

CELLO

17th Century English Carol
Music from W. Sandys' *Christmas Carols*

Copyright © 2006 by HAL LEONARD CORPORATION
International Copyright Secured All Rights Reserved

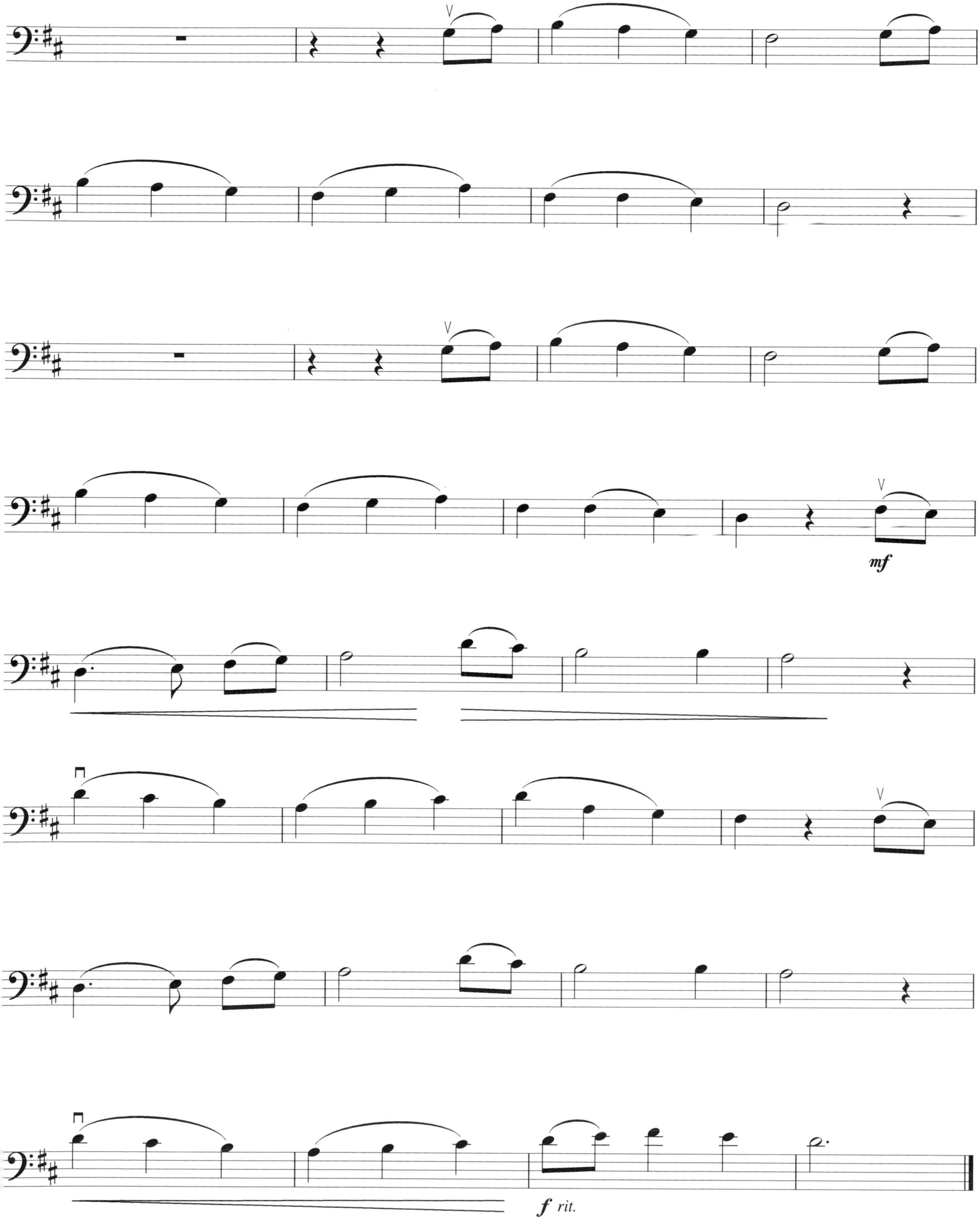
mf
f rit.

GOOD CHRISTIAN MEN, REJOICE

CELLO

14th Century Latin Text
14th Century German Melody

Copyright © 2006 by HAL LEONARD CORPORATION
International Copyright Secured All Rights Reserved

GOOD KING WENCESLAS

CELLO

Words by JOHN M. NEALE
Music from *Piae Cantiones*

Copyright © 2006 by HAL LEONARD CORPORATION
International Copyright Secured All Rights Reserved

HARK! THE HERALD ANGELS SING

CELLO

Words by CHARLES WESLEY
Music by FELIX MENDELSSOHN-BARTHOLDY

Copyright © 2006 by HAL LEONARD CORPORATION
International Copyright Secured All Rights Reserved

I HEARD THE BELLS ON CHRISTMAS DAY

CELLO

Words by HENRY WADSWORTH LONGFELLOW
Music by JOHN BAPTISTE CALKIN

Copyright © 2006 by HAL LEONARD CORPORATION
International Copyright Secured All Rights Reserved

IT CAME UPON THE MIDNIGHT CLEAR

CELLO

Words by EDMUND HAMILTON SEARS
Music by RICHARD STORRS WILLIS

Copyright © 2006 by HAL LEONARD CORPORATION
International Copyright Secured All Rights Reserved

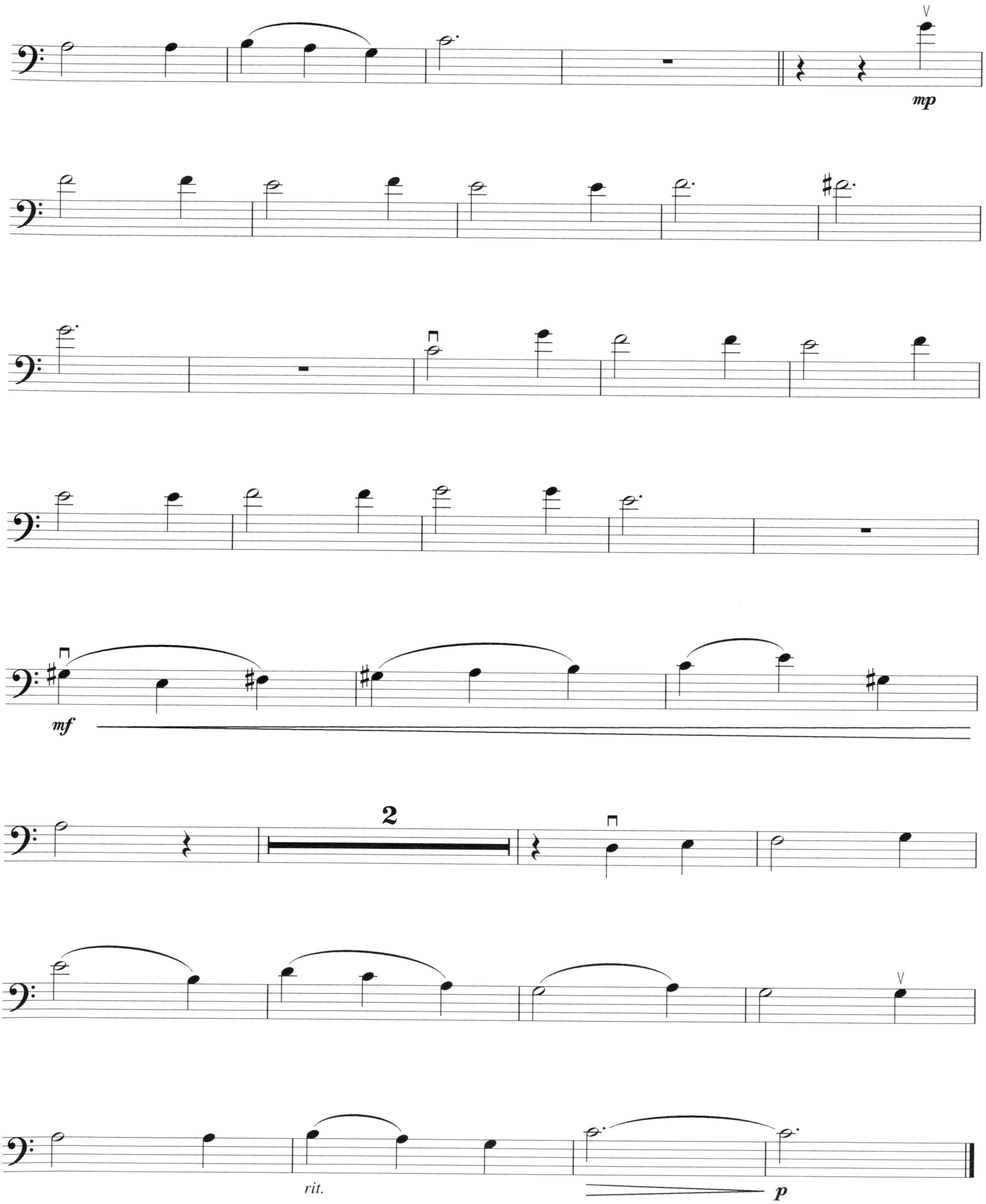
mp
mf
2
rit.
p

JOY TO THE WORLD

CELLO

Words by ISAAC WATTS
Music by GEORGE FRIDERIC HANDEL

Copyright © 2006 by HAL LEONARD CORPORATION
International Copyright Secured All Rights Reserved

f
f
mf
f
ff

O CHRISTMAS TREE

CELLO

Traditional German Carol

Copyright © 2006 by HAL LEONARD CORPORATION
International Copyright Secured All Rights Reserved

O COME, O COME, EMMANUEL

CELLO

Plainsong, 13th Century

Copyright © 2006 by HAL LEONARD CORPORATION
International Copyright Secured All Rights Reserved

SING WE NOW OF CHRISTMAS

CELLO

Traditional

Copyright © 2006 by HAL LEONARD CORPORATION
International Copyright Secured   All Rights Reserved

mf
f
mp
ff

WE THREE KINGS OF ORIENT ARE

CELLO

Words and Music by
JOHN H. HOPKINS, JR.

Copyright © 2006 by HAL LEONARD CORPORATION
International Copyright Secured All Rights Reserved

f
mf
mp
f
mp
mf
rit.

WE WISH YOU A MERRY CHRISTMAS

CELLO

Traditional English Folksong

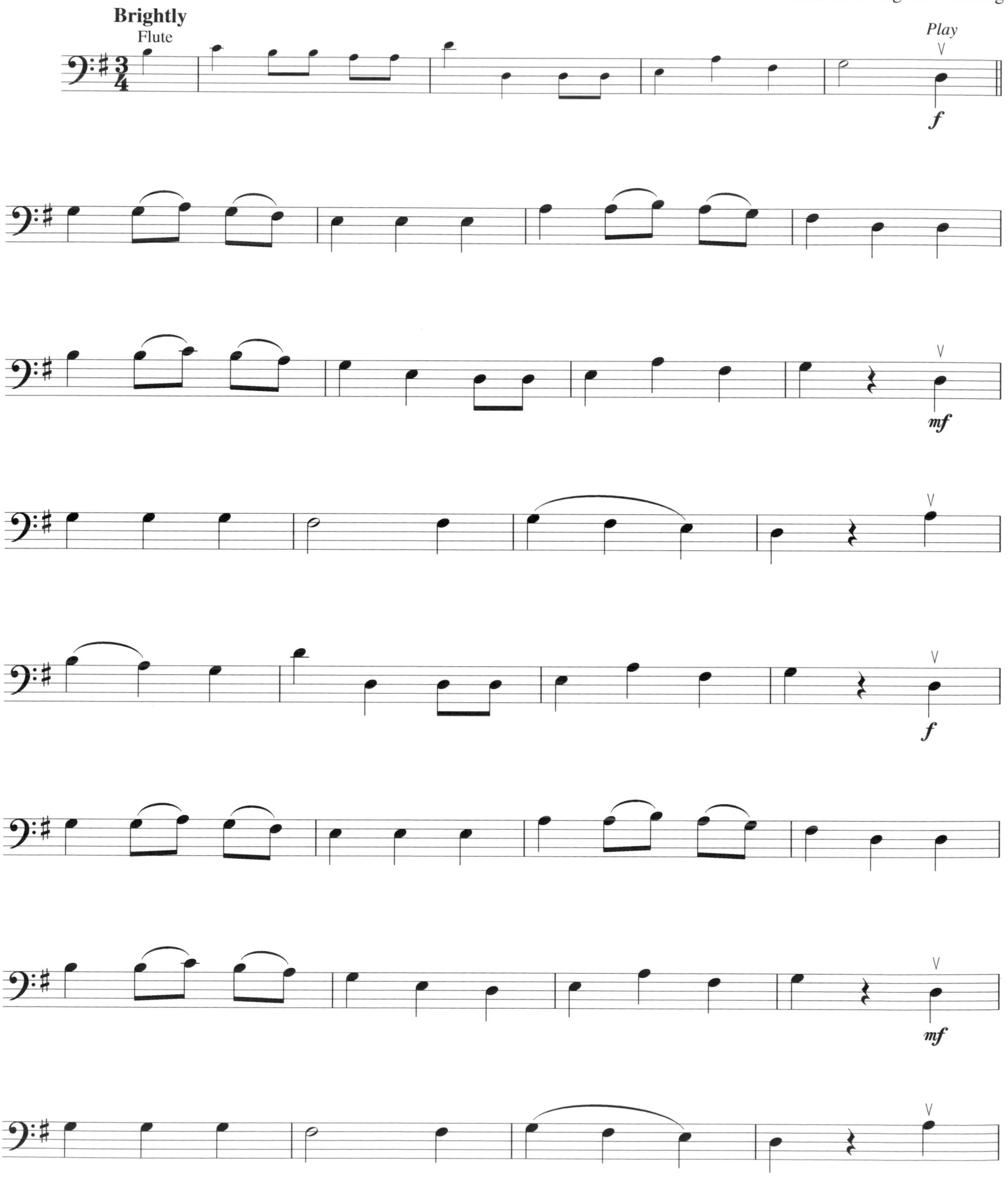

Copyright © 2006 by HAL LEONARD CORPORATION
International Copyright Secured All Rights Reserved

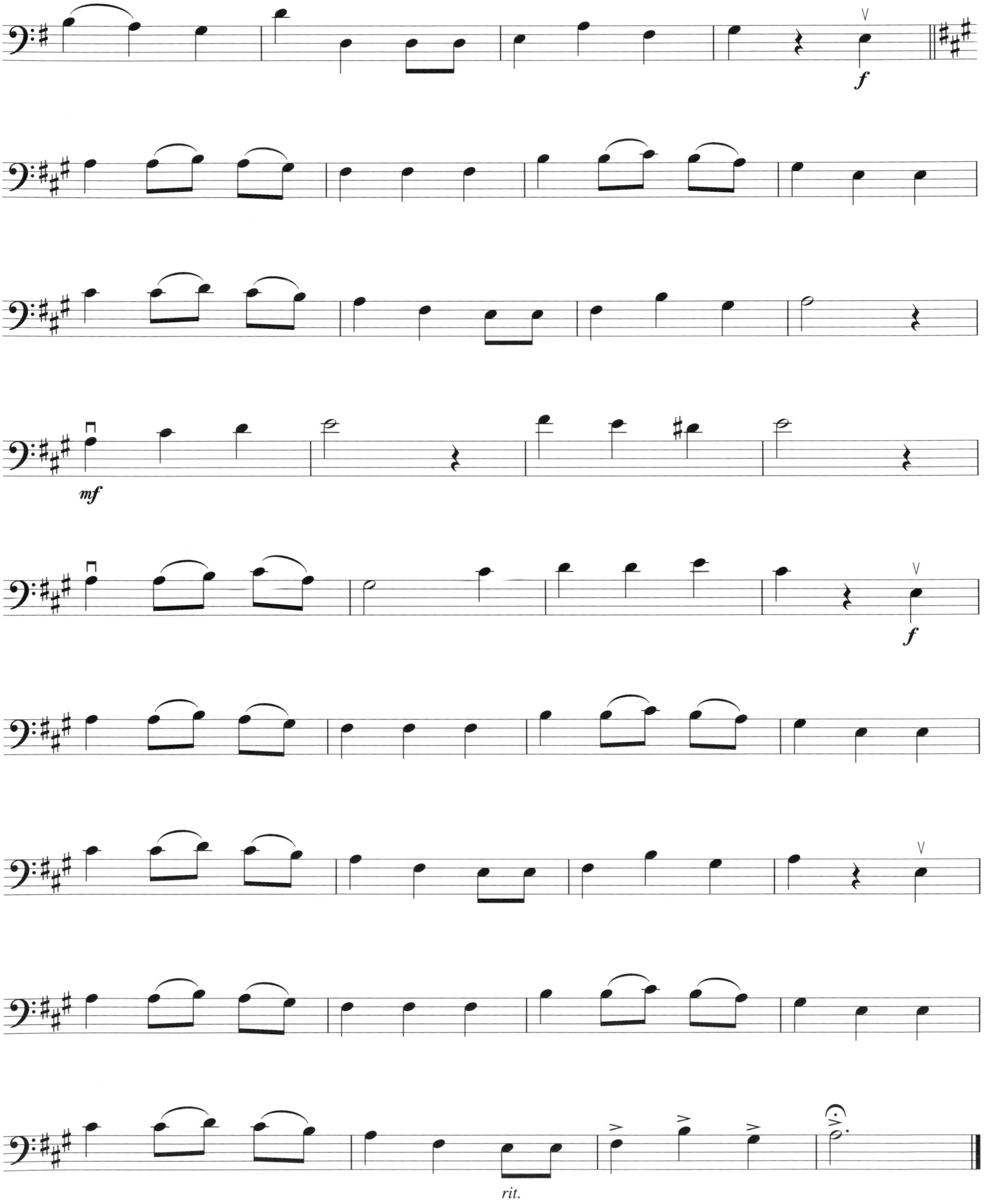
f
mf
f
rit.

O LITTLE TOWN OF BETHLEHEM

CELLO

Words by PHILLIPS BROOKS
Music by LEWIS H. REDNER

Copyright © 2006 by HAL LEONARD CORPORATION
International Copyright Secured All Rights Reserved

HAL•LEONARD INSTRUMENTAL PLAY-ALONG

Your favorite songs are arranged just for solo instrumentalists with this outstanding series. Each book includes great full-accompaniment play-along audio so you can sound just like a pro!

Check out **halleonard.com** for songlists, more titles, or to order online from your favorite music retailer.

12 Pop Hits
12 songs • $14.99 each
00261790 Flute 00261795 Horn
00261791 Clarinet 00261796 Trombone
00261792 Alto Sax 00261797 Violin
00261793 Tenor Sax 00261798 Viola
00261794 Trumpet 00261799 Cello

The Very Best of Bach
15 selections • $12.99 each
00225371 Flute 00225376 Horn
00225372 Clarinet 00225377 Trombone
00225373 Alto Sax 00225378 Violin
00225374 Tenor Sax 00225379 Viola
00225375 Trumpet 00225380 Cello

The Beatles
15 songs • $14.99 each
00225330 Flute 00225335 Horn
00225331 Clarinet 00225336 Trombone
00225332 Alto Sax 00225337 Violin
00225333 Tenor Sax 00225338 Viola
00225334 Trumpet 00225339 Cello

Chart Hits
12 songs • $14.99 each
00146207 Flute 00146212 Horn
00146208 Clarinet 00146213 Trombone
00146209 Alto Sax 00146214 Violin
00146210 Tenor Sax 00146215 Viola
00146211 Trumpet 00146216 Cello

Christmas Songs
12 songs • $12.99 each
00146855 Flute 00146863 Horn
00146858 Clarinet 00146864 Trombone
00146859 Alto Sax 00146866 Violin
00146860 Tenor Sax 00146867 Viola
00146862 Trumpet 00146868 Cello

Contemporary Broadway
15 songs • $14.99 each
00298704 Flute 00298709 Horn
00298705 Clarinet 00298710 Trombone
00298706 Alto Sax 00298711 Violin
00298707 Tenor Sax 00298712 Viola
00298708 Trumpet 00298713 Cello

Disney Movie Hits
12 songs • $14.99 each
00841420 Flute 00841424 Horn
00841687 Oboe 00841425 Trombone
00841421 Clarinet 00841426 Violin
00841422 Alto Sax 00841427 Viola
00841686 Tenor Sax 00841428 Cello
00841423 Trumpet

Prices, contents, and availability subject to change without notice.

Disney characters and artwork ™ & © 2021 Disney

Disney Solos
12 songs • $14.99 each
00841404 Flute 00841506 Oboe
00841406 Alto Sax 0841409 Trumpet
00841407 Horn 00841410 Violin
00841411 Viola 00841412 Cello
00841405 Clarinet/Tenor Sax
00841408 Trombone/Baritone
00841553 Mallet Percussion

Dixieland Favorites
15 songs • $12.99 each
00268756 Flute 0068759 Trumpet
00268757 Clarinet 00268760 Trombone
00268758 Alto Sax

Billie Eilish
9 songs • $14.99 each
00345648 Flute 00345653 Horn
00345649 Clarinet 00345654 Trombone
00345650 Alto Sax 00345655 Violin
00345651 Tenor Sax 00345656 Viola
00345652 Trumpet 00345657 Cello

Favorite Movie Themes
13 songs • $14.99 each
00841166 Flute 00841168 Trumpet
00841167 Clarinet 00841170 Trombone
00841169 Alto Sax 00841296 Violin

Gospel Hymns
15 songs • $12.99 each
00194648 Flute 00194654 Trombone
00194649 Clarinet 00194655 Violin
00194650 Alto Sax 00194656 Viola
00194651 Tenor Sax 00194657 Cello
00194652 Trumpet

Great Classical Themes
15 songs • $12.99 each
00292727 Flute 00292733 Horn
00292728 Clarinet 00292735 Trombone
00292729 Alto Sax 00292736 Violin
00292730 Tenor Sax 00292737 Viola
00292732 Trumpet 00292738 Cello

The Greatest Showman
8 songs • $14.99 each
00277389 Flute 00277394 Horn
00277390 Clarinet 00277395 Trombone
00277391 Alto Sax 00277396 Violin
00277392 Tenor Sax 00277397 Viola
00277393 Trumpet 00277398 Cello

Irish Favorites
31 songs • $12.99 each
00842489 Flute 00842495 Trombone
00842490 Clarinet 00842496 Violin
00842491 Alto Sax 00842497 Viola
00842493 Trumpet 00842498 Cello
00842494 Horn

Michael Jackson
11 songs • $14.99 each
00119495 Flute 00119499 Trumpet
00119496 Clarinet 00119501 Trombone
00119497 Alto Sax 00119503 Violin
00119498 Tenor Sax 00119502 Accomp.

Jazz & Blues
14 songs • $14.99 each
00841438 Flute 00841441 Trumpet
00841439 Clarinet 00841443 Trombone
00841440 Alto Sax 00841444 Violin
00841442 Tenor Sax

Jazz Classics
12 songs • $12.99 each
00151812 Flute 00151816 Trumpet
00151813 Clarinet 00151818 Trombone
00151814 Alto Sax 00151819 Violin
00151815 Tenor Sax 00151821 Cello

Les Misérables
13 songs • $14.99 each
00842292 Flute 00842297 Horn
00842293 Clarinet 00842298 Trombone
00842294 Alto Sax 00842299 Violin
00842295 Tenor Sax 00842300 Viola
00842296 Trumpet 00842301 Cello

Metallica
12 songs • $14.99 each
02501327 Flute 02502454 Horn
02501339 Clarinet 02501329 Trombone
02501332 Alto Sax 02501334 Violin
02501333 Tenor Sax 02501335 Viola
02501330 Trumpet 02501338 Cello

Motown Classics
15 songs • $12.99 each
00842572 Flute 00842576 Trumpet
00842573 Clarinet 00842578 Trombone
00842574 Alto Sax 00842579 Violin
00842575 Tenor Sax

Pirates of the Caribbean
16 songs • $14.99 each
00842183 Flute 00842188 Horn
00842184 Clarinet 00842189 Trombone
00842185 Alto Sax 00842190 Violin
00842186 Tenor Sax 00842191 Viola
00842187 Trumpet 00842192 Cello

Queen
17 songs • $14.99 each
00285402 Flute 00285407 Horn
00285403 Clarinet 00285408 Trombone
00285404 Alto Sax 00285409 Violin
00285405 Tenor Sax 00285410 Viola
00285406 Trumpet 00285411 Cello

Simple Songs
14 songs • $12.99 each
00249081 Flute 00249087 Horn
00249092 Oboe 00249089 Trombone
00249082 Clarinet 00249090 Violin
00249083 Alto Sax 00249091 Viola
00249084 Tenor Sax 00249092 Cello
00249086 Trumpet 00249094 Mallets

Superhero Themes
14 songs • $14.99 each
00363195 Flute 00363200 Horn
00363196 Clarinet 00363201 Trombone
00363197 Alto Sax 00363202 Violin
00363198 Tenor Sax 00363203 Viola
00363199 Trumpet 00363204 Cello

Star Wars
16 songs • $16.99 each
00350900 Flute 00350907 Horn
00350913 Oboe 00350908 Trombone
00350903 Clarinet 00330909 Violin
00350904 Alto Sax 00350910 Viola
00350905 Tenor Sax 00350911 Cello
00350906 Trumpet 00350914 Mallet

Taylor Swift
15 songs • $12.99 each
00842532 Flute 00842537 Horn
00842533 Clarinet 00842538 Trombone
00842534 Alto Sax 00842539 Violin
00842535 Tenor Sax 00842540 Viola
00842536 Trumpet 00842541 Cello

Video Game Music
13 songs • $12.99 each
00283877 Flute 00283883 Horn
00283878 Clarinet 00283884 Trombone
00283879 Alto Sax 00283885 Violin
00283880 Tenor Sax 00283886 Viola
00283882 Trumpet 00283887 Cello

Wicked
13 songs • $12.99 each
00842236 Flute 00842241 Horn
00842237 Clarinet 00842242 Trombone
00842238 Alto Sax 00842243 Violin
00842239 Tenor Sax 00842244 Viola
00842240 Trumpet 00842245 Cello

HAL•LEONARD®

0521
488